SOUTH WALES BUSES IN THE 1990s

KEITH A. JENKINSON

AMBERLEY

First published 2022

Amberley Publishing
The Hill, Stroud
Gloucestershire, GL5 4EP

www.amberley-books.com

Copyright © Keith A. Jenkinson, 2022

The right of Keith A. Jenkinson to be identified
as the Author of this work has been asserted in
accordance with the Copyrights, Designs and
Patents Act 1988.

ISBN 978 1 4456 9714 7 (print)
ISBN 978 1 4456 9715 4 (ebook)

British Library Cataloguing in Publication Data.
A catalogue record for this book is available from
the British Library.

Origination by Amberley Publishing.
Printed in the UK.

Introduction

In the twentieth century, bus and coach services in South Wales were maintained by a fascinating mixture of municipal undertakings, large national groups, and numerous independent operators, but in more recent times the scene has changed dramatically with administrative changes, takeovers, deregulation, newcomers, and the disappearance of several old established companies.

In 1967, BET subsidiary Western Welsh Omnibus Company was sold to the state-owned Transport Holding Company and then, two years later, became part of the National Bus Company. Upon a reorganisation in 1971/72, Western Welsh transferred its operations west of Bridgend to NBC subsidiaries South Wales Transport and Crosville, and in return took over Rhondda Transport, itself a former BET company. Meanwhile, in 1969 the erstwhile BET companies Thomas Bros, Port Talbot and Neath & Cardiff Luxury Coaches were merged into South Wales Transport, as too was former Tilling Group United Welsh Services in 1971.

Then, in April 1974, as a consequence of major local government reorganisation, several councils were renamed or merged together, with Aberdare UDC becoming Cynon Valley District Council; Bedwas & Machen, Caerphilly, and Gelligaer UDCs combining to form Rhymney Valley District Council; Pontypridd UDC became Taff Ely Borough Council; and West Monmouthshire Omnibus Board was swallowed into Islwyn Borough Council, which itself was abolished in 1996 when it became part of Caerphilly County Borough. This eventually led to all the old municipalities' buses established liveries and identities being replaced by new colour schemes and fleet names to leave only the Cardiff and Newport undertakings unchanged.

More changes were implemented in April 1978 when the NBC transferred Red & White Services to Western Welsh and renamed the merged company National Welsh Services Ltd. In the 1980, however, the Red & White fleet name was reintroduced on services operating in the eastern part of National Welsh's territory.

When deregulation came about in debut in October 1986, several new independent operators joined those already established in the local bus market and began to flex their muscles against the NBC and municipal companies with mixed degrees of success. Among the early newcomers was Clayton Jones, Pontypridd, who grew to become one of the largest south-east Wales independents before selling out to Veolia in 2006 and then briefly starting up again. To name all the independent operators in South Wales who took advantage of deregulation would take a book of its own, but many will be seen in the photographs that follow. Among the first casualties, however, were old established Creamline Services, Tonmawr, who ceased operating in January 1987; Peakes, Pontypool, who during the following months sold its bus operations to National Welsh; and Capitol, Cwmbran, who sold its Cardiff-based Morris Bros operation to Caerphilly Travel Centre.

In addition to the above, in May 1987 National Welsh and South Wales Transport were both sold by the NBC to their respective management (South Wales Transport adopting the name United Welsh Group) and in 1988 National Welsh introduced a new red, white and green livery. Also in 1988, United Welsh Group expanded by purchasing the old established business of Brewers, Caerau, which it retained as a separate subsidiary; Llynfi, Maesteg; and Swansea-based

Morris. Davies Bros, Pencader bought the twelve-bus business of Eynons, Trimsaran, and National Welsh acquired the municipal bus operation of Taff Ely.

The number of municipal bus operators further shrank in February 1989 when National Welsh purchased Rhymey Valley District Council's arm's length eighty-three-vehicle Inter Valley Link company. Following this, in July 1989 Merthyr Tydfil Transport passed into administration after failing to find a buyer, and ceased trading during the following month.

Further changes took place in 1990, the first of which was the sale in February of South Wales Transport, Brewers, and United Welsh Coaches, along with their 350 vehicles, to the Badgerline Group, who four months later purchased DLJ Private Hire, Maesteg, but immediately sold all of its fifteen coaches. Then, in January 1991, National Welsh sold its eastern operations (Red & White) to Western Travel, who owned former NBC Cheltenham & Gloucester. Later in the year, in November Capitol Coaches, Cwmbran, took over the remnants of old established Hills of Tredegar, who had passed into receivership two months earlier.

In February 1992 National Welsh, whose struggles continued to grow, sold its Porth, Aberdare and Merthyr Tydfil depots to a new consortium trading as Rhondda Buses, who quickly resold its Aberdare and Merthyr Tydfil depots, operations, and forty-six buses to Offerdemo, a company owned by Cynon Valley Transport directors, while Rhondda added National Welsh's Caerphilly depot to its portfolio. Meanwhile, Offerdemo quickly closed its Aberdare depot as this was competing with Cynon Valley's services and thus presented its directors with a conflict of interest. Then, as no buyer could be found for National Welsh's Bridgend depot, it was closed, leaving only Barry depot continuing to operate. Now run by the administrators, hopes were pinned on an employee buyout, and although this was formed under the name Barry Line Bus Company and gained an operators licence for 165 vehicles, it sadly floundered before it began, resulting in Barry depot being closed in July, leaving Cardiff City Transport as the main provider of the town's bus services, and National Welsh finally passing into oblivion. Later, in August 1992 the Offerdomo operation also closed down, and during the same month, to further strengthen its portfolio, Red & White purchased Cynon Valley Transport.

During the following year, Rhondda Buses acquired fifteen-bus independent Cyril Evans of Senghenydd in May, while four months later Tellings Golden Miller started local bus operations in Cardiff with second-hand double-deckers under the Cardiff Bluebird name. Then, during the final month of the year, Stagecoach purchased Western Travel, giving it its first foray into Wales.

After Cardiff-based Wheadons Coaches' purchase of fifteen-vehicle Greyhound Coaches, also of Cardiff, in November 1994, the year that followed proved to be far more eventful with Golden Coaches, Llantwit Major, closing in February and passing its services to Cardiff Bus and, two months later, Rhondda Buses acquiring Parfitts Motor Services, Rhymney Bridge, together with its forty-seven buses. During this same month, D Coaches of Morriston purchased twenty-seven-vehicle Glantawe Coaches, Pontardawe, but retained its name, while in May Badgerline and GRT merged to form FirstBus, with South Wales Transport, Brewers and United Welsh Coaches now passing to the new giant, who ultimately adopted the title First Cymru. Later, in October Brewers took over Cardiff City Transport's four-vehicle coaching unit and its Vale Busline operations, which were based on the former Golden Coaches services. Finally, Rhondda Buses continued to use the Parfitts and Caerphilly Busways names on a number of its buses.

The year 1996 began in January with Jones' Pontypridd-based Shamrock purchasing eleven-vehicle Thomas of Barry and ten-vehicle Truemans of Pontypool to make it South Wales's largest independent operator with a total fleet of 130 buses and coaches, while in April Evans Coaches of New Tredegar ceased operating, having been established since the end of the First World War. A further departure from the scene came in September when Cardiff Bluebird closed its operation and sold its forty-two vehicles to Cardiff City Transport, who disposed of them without further use.

Moving forward to 1997, during the final month of that year Stagecoach expanded its Welsh portfolio when it purchased Rhondda Buses, whose fleet numbered 100 vehicles, and quickly merged these into its Red & White operation. Then, during the latter months of the following year, a new operator, Alister's Coaches, began some services in Cardiff and Barry using elderly minibuses. In a bid to rid itself of this new competition, Cardiff Bus launched Ely Value Bus – also using minibuses – and after a lengthy battle, Alister's conceded defeat in June 1999 and withdrew from the scene. During this same month, old established Davies of Pencader sadly went into receivership but was quickly bought by First Cymru along with its thirty-eight vehicles.

Although this book does not include the changes that took place in the twenty-first century, before closing it is worthy to note that in January 2000 Shamrock Travel, Pontypridd, acquired sixteen-vehicle Venture Travel of Cardiff, who, after being retained as a subsidiary, purchased Stevens Travel, Newport, in May, while in September Stagecoach further strengthened its position with the acquisition of the bus operations and twenty-eight buses of Phil Anslow of Pontypool, who continued in business as a coach operator. At this time, only three municipal operators remained, and while Cardiff and Newport are still going strong today, Islwyn Borough Transport ceased in January 2010 when it was acquired by Stagecoach.

As will be seen in the following pages, South Wales was – and still is, of course, – a fascinating area for all those with an interest in buses and coaches. It is hoped that this book will give a small insight into an ever-changing scene.

Pictured in Cardiff bus station in February 1971 after its transfer from United Welsh to South Wales Transport, and displaying its new fleet name, is ECW-bodied Bristol RELL6G 604 (CWN 624C), which was new in July 1965. (Author's collection)

Resting in its home town in August 1971 is Porthcawl Omnibus Co.'s scruffy ex-London Transport RT-type AEC LYR 875, still in its previous operator's livery. (K. A. Jenkinson)

Awaiting its next duty to Carmarthen in February 1972 is Eynon of Trimsaran's Weymann-bodied Leyland Tiger Cub NNY 58, which began life with Thomas, Port Talbot, in 1954. (K. A. Jenkinson)

Parked in the yard of South Wales Transport's Llanelli depot on 1 February 1972 are two of the company's AEC Regent Vs – 257 (281 DWN) and 256 (280 DNY) – which carried low-height single-deck Roe bodies to enable them to pass under low bridges at the town's docks. (K. A. Jenkinson)

Painted in Western Welsh dual-purpose livery, Willowbrook-bodied Leyland Leopard 1507 is seen here in Cardiff bus station in February 1973. (K. A. Jenkinson)

New to United Welsh in December 1957, but seen here in Pontardawe in February 1973 used by South Wales Transport as a driver trainer, is ECW-bodied Bristol LD6G OCY 959. (K. A. Jenkinson)

Among the buses resting outside their Sloper Road depot in February 1973 are Cardiff City Transport East Lancs-bodied Leyland PD3A/30 400 (400 BUH) and one of the undertaking's AEC Regent Vs. (K. A. Jenkinson)

Seen in the yard of its Blackwood depot in February 1973 are several of West Monmouthshire Omnibus Board's Weymann-bodied Leyland Tiger Cubs, including 2 (125 BAX), and others in their owner's new colours, and withdrawn ex-Western Welsh Weymann-bodied Leyland Tiger Cub 17 (JBO 117) still in the old livery. (K. A. Jenkinson)

Seen taking a break between duties at its depot in February 1973 is one of Gelligaer UDC's Longwell Green-bodied AEC Reliances. (K. A. Jenkinson)

New to Western Welsh in November 1965, Park Royal-bodied Leyland Tiger Cub FUH 363C is seen at its owner's Ely workshops in February 1973 after being repainted for its transfer to Crosville, in whose fleet it was numbered STL939. (K. A. Jenkinson)

Cardiff City Transport's dual-door Alexander-bodied AEC Swift 516 (MBO 516F), which was new in June 1968 and sports a pay as you enter sign below its windscreen, is seen here passing Cardiff Castle in March 1973. (K. A. Jenkinson)

Standing at Talbot Green waiting its next duty in March 1973 is Rhondda's Willowbrook-bodied Leyland Tiger Cub 2387 (387 WTG). (K. A. Jenkinson)

Entering its open-air depot is Llynfi, Maesteg, ex-Glasgow Corporation Alexander-bodied Leyland PDR1/1 136 (AGA 129B), while in the yard to the left are several other members of the Llynfi fleet. (John Law)

South Wales Transport were great lovers of AEC Regent Vs, one of which – Willowbrook-bodied 894 (GWN 872E), new in January 1967 – is seen here in Swansea bus station in NBC days. (Author's collection)

New to Thames Valley and passing to Morris Bros, Swansea, in August 1980, ECW-bodied Bristol FLF6G GRX 140D is seen here after being preserved and restored. (F. W. York)

Displaying a South Wales fleet name and painted in corporate National Express livery, Willowbrook-bodied Leyland Leopard 110 (LCY 110X) is seen here heading to Swansea. (F. W. York)

Seen in its home town bus station is Merthyr Tydfil Transport's Duple-bodied Leyland Leopard 234 (OWO 234Y), which had been purchased new in September 1982. (K. A. Jenkinson)

Merthyr Tydfil Transport Leyland Lynx 111 (D111 NDW), which was new in July 1987, only had a short life with its original owner before being sold to London Borough of Hillingdon in 1989. (K. A. Jenkinson)

Heading along Glyndwr Road past Cwmbran bus station on a local service on 16 March 1994 is Phil Anslow Travel's coach-seated Made to Measure-bodied Mercedes Benz 811D F615 FNA, which began life with Flavin, Stanford-le-Hope, in November 1988. (K. A. Jenkinson)

Seen here with Inter Valley Link in 1989, en route to Merthyr Tydfil, is ex-Midland Red North Marshall-bodied Leyland Leopard 1101 (SHA 639N), which started life in October 1974. (K. A. Jenkinson)

Departing from Caerphilly bus station on route 27 to Graig-y-Rhacca, and painted in Caerphilly Buslink livery, is National Welsh Leyland National N654 (BUH 219V). (K. A. Jenkinson)

Carrying Tripper branding on its side panels is Merthyr Tydfil Transport MCW Metrorider 502 (F502 ANY), seen here on a journey to the town's hospital in March 1989. (K. A. Jenkinson)

Caught by the camera in April 1989 when only a few weeks old, Cardiff Bus Leyland Lynx 240 (F240 CNY) is seen here operating the 12 service to Ely. (K. A. Jenkinson)

New in July 1978 and converted to open-top configuration in July 1986, National Welsh ECW-bodied Bristol VRT HR818 (VHB 678S) stands in Cardiff bus station before working the X99 service to Barry Island in 1989. In April of the following year it was sold to Crosville, and is now preserved. (K. A. Jenkinson)

New to Manchester Minibuses in January 1987, and seen here two years later after their purchase by Cardiff Bus, are Carlyle-converted Freight Rover Sherpas D66 (D107 NOJ) and D67 (D131 NON). (K. A. Jenkinson)

Thomas of Barry's smartly presented Leyland National JHU864L, seen here in Cardiff in October 1989, began life with Bristol Omnibus Company in July 1973. (K. A. Jenkinson)

Newport Transport's East Lancs-bodied Dodge S56 7 (D807 MNY) passes through the centre of its home town followed by two of the undertaking's Marshall-bodied Scania BR112DHs with 100 (PTG 100Y) being closest to the camera. (K. A. Jenkinson)

Cardiff Bus Willowbrook-bodied Bristol VRT 302 (SWO 302S), with three youthful passengers at the front of the upper deck, is seen here on a journey to its home city's Central station. (K. A. Jenkinson)

Painted in 'Classic' livery, Inter Valley Link MCW Metrorider 106 (F106 YWO) is seen here taking a rest between its duties. (K. A. Jenkinson)

Cardiff Bus PMT-bodied Mercedes Benz L608D 111 (D111 LTG), which was purchased new in September 1986, is seen here in 1989 sporting a Cardiff Minibus fleet name and Pick an Orange strapline. (K. A. Jenkinson)

Passing through its home town is Newport Transport's East Lancs-bodied Scania N112DRB 30 (C30 ETG). (K. A. Jenkinson)

Cardiff Bus's convertible open-top Alexander-bodied Bristol VRT 359 (WTG 259T) is seen here on a typical wet day, with its roof removed, operating a sightseeing tour of its home city. (K. A. Jenkinson)

Heading into Pontypridd is Cynon Valley 2 (E292 TAX), a dual-purpose-seated Northern Counties-bodied Renault S56 that was new in March 1988. (K. A. Jenkinson)

National Welsh Carlyle-bodied Freight Rover Sherpa 96 (E96 OUH) is about to be overtaken by Robin Hood-converted (on a Dormobile shell) Ford Transit 15 (C115 HUH), both of which are painted in their owner's Bustler livery. (K. A. Jenkinson)

Seen in Pontypridd is National Welsh Carlyle-bodied Freight Rover Sherpa 226 (F226 AWO), which was new in November 1988 and carries a Taff Ely Bustler fleet name, while behind it is a sister vehicle painted in the old Bustler livery. (K. A. Jenkinson)

Cardiff Bus Northern Counties-bodied Ailsa B55 416 (NDW 416X) stands alongside East Lancs-bodied Leyland Olympian 518 (A518 VKG) in their home city's bus station. (K. A. Jenkinson)

Looking somewhat careworn is C. K. Coaches', Cardiff, Metro Cammell-bodied Leyland PDR1/2 DAU 425C, which began life with Nottingham City Transport in May 1965. (Author's collection)

Sporting a Shamrock Coaches fleet name, Pontypridd-based Clayton Jones' Duple-bodied Dennis Javelin F362 SAY, which was purchased new in June 1989, is seen here on a private hire duty. (K. A. Jenkinson)

Seen here in Cardiff bus station in September 1990, still wearing the livery and fleet name of its previous owner, Premier Travel, Cambridge, is Golden Coaches of Llantwit Major's Plaxton-bodied AEC Reliance PCE 601R. (K. A. Jenkinson)

Heading to Gatwick is National Welsh's National Express-liveried Plaxton Paramount 3200-bodied Leyland Tiger UC1203 (SDW 919Y), which was new in May 1983. (T. W. W. Knowles)

Seen operating a private hire duty in September 1990 is D Coaches of Morriston's Plaxton-bodied DAF MB200 (ACY 46D). (K. A. Jenkinson)

Reversing off the stand in Swansea bus station on the 110 service to Burry Port is South Wales Transport Reeve Burgess-bodied Mercedes Benz 709D 311 (F311 AWN), which carries SosbanLink branding on its side panels. (K. A. Jenkinson)

South Wales Transport MCW Metrorider 271 (E271 REP), which was new in August 1987, is seen here in Swansea bus station fitted with advertising boards around its roof edge. After leaving South Wales, it joined the fleet of GM Buses North. (K. A. Jenkinson)

Displaying branding for the Cityrunner service between Carmarthen and Swansea is South Wales Transport Phoenix-bodied Mercedes Benz 0814D 369 (G368 MEP), which was new in June 1990. (K. A. Jenkinson)

New to National Welsh in September 1980 and seen here ten years later, low-height ECW-bodied Bristol VRT LR715 (GTX 739W) prepares to leave Cardiff bus station on an X26 journey to Llanbradach. (K. A. Jenkinson)

Still wearing NBC poppy red and white livery and seen here in Cardiff bus station, National Welsh ECW-bodied Bristol VRT HR804 (SKG 898S) began life in September 1977 with Western Welsh. (K. A. Jenkinson)

Purchased new by Bebb Travel, Llantwit Fardre, in January 1990, Carlyle-bodied Freight Rover Sherpa G34 HDW is seen here in Cardiff later that year. (K. A. Jenkinson)

Collecting some passengers in Cardiff bus station in September 1990 is Red & White Leyland National 414 (KDW 360P), which started life with Western Welsh in November 1975. (K. A. Jenkinson)

Passengers board Merthyr-bound National Welsh dual-purpose Willowbrook-bodied Leyland Leopard UD387 (KWO 556X) in Cardiff bus station in July 1991. (K. A. Jenkinson)

New to Aberdare UDC in September 1972, which became Cynon Valley BC two years later, ECW-bodied Bristol RESL LTG40L was in November 1989 sold to Golden Coaches, Llantwit Major, with whom it is seen here in Cardiff bus station. Withdrawn in July 1993, it was disposed of for scrap in December 1994. (K. A. Jenkinson)

Seen here in Cardiff bus station, National Welsh ECW-bodied Leyland Olympian HR853 (MUH 283X) was sold to Southend Transport in October 1992, then passed to Arriva East Herts & Essex, and in 2002 to Roundabout Buses, Copthorne. (K. A. Jenkinson)

Still in NBC poppy red livery and displaying the slogan 'Serving the communities of South Wales' on its cove panels, Red & White Leyland National N596 (SKG 906S) deposits its passengers in Cardiff bus station in June 1991. (K. A. Jenkinson)

Wearing Rhondda Buses new livery, and seen here in Cardiff bus station, is Leyland National 435 (NOW 469R), which began life with Western Welsh in March 1977. (K. A. Jenkinson)

New in November 1975 to NBC subsidiary Jones, Aberbeeg, Leyland National ND401 (KDW 347P) became part of the National Welsh fleet before its transfer to Rhondda, with whom it is seen here depositing its passengers in Cardiff bus station in July 1991. (K. A. Jenkinson)

Seen in Cardiff bus station in August 1991, branded for the Shuttle service to Swansea pioneered by Neath & Cardiff Luxury Coaches in the 1930s, is South Wales Transport's ECW coach-bodied Leyland Olympian 909 (B696 BPU), which started life with Eastern National in May 1985. (K. A. Jenkinson)

Pictured in Cardiff bus station in June 1991 adorned with Swiftlink branding, National Welsh ECW-bodied Leyland Leopard 895 (AAX 563A) was originally registered PKG 106Y. (K. A. Jenkinson)

Operating the 550 service from Cardigan to Aberystwyth is Richard Bros of Moylgrove's Duple Dominant-bodied Bedford YLQ LDE 547P, which was purchased new in May 1976. (T. W. W. Knowles)

Starting life with National Welsh in September 1980, ECW-bodied Bristol VRT GTX 741W is seen here in Cardiff bus station in June 1991 wearing Rhondda Buses livery. (K. A. Jenkinson)

Carlyle Dailybus-bodied Iveco 49.10 H859 NOC began life as a Carlyle demonstrator in April 1991, and is seen here later that year in Swansea before ultimately being purchased by Wright, Wrexham. (K. A. Jenkinson)

Reversing off its stand in Swansea bus station at the start of its journey to Port Talbot in August 1991 is South Wales Transport Robin Hood-bodied Mercedes Benz 814D 361 (G361 JTH), which carries Valley Link branding on its side panels. (K. A. Jenkinson)

Making its way through Cardiff en route to Pontypridd in July 1991 is Clayton Jones' Shamrock Shoppa Made to Measure-bodied Mercedes Benz 709D H690 UHH, which had been purchased new four months earlier. (K. A. Jenkinson)

Leaving Swansea bus station on a journey to Pembroke Dock in August 1991 is Davies Bros of Trimsaran's ECW-bodied Leyland Tiger 196 (WPH 136Y), which was new to London Country and ultimately ended its life with Northern Bus, Anston. (K. A. Jenkinson)

Starting life with Rhymney Valley DC in March 1981, and later passing to Inter Valley Link and then National Welsh, in whose livery it is seen here in Cardiff in July 1991 with Rhondda fleet names, East Lancs-bodied Bristol VRT 828 (GHB 84W) later operated for Forest, Bootle and Mercury, Hoo, before being scrapped in June 1998. (K. A. Jenkinson)

Passengers wait in Cardiff bus station in May 1991 to board National Welsh Leyland National N611 (PKG 743R), which was new to Western Welsh in May 1977 and is seen here preparing to undertake a journey to Porthcawl via Bridgend. (K. A. Jenkinson)

New to Southern Vectis, and seen here in Swansea in August 1991, ECW-bodied Bristol RELL6G TDL 566K had migrated to Wales in July 1988 when it was acquired by Atlas, Gorseinon, and then passed to Hawkes, Waurarlwydd, who traded as City Connection, before entering preservation in 2002. Unfortunately, however, it was sold for scrap in February 2012. (K. A. Jenkinson)

Seen in Cardiff bus station in July 1991, about to depart to Abergavenny, is freshly repainted Red & White ECW-bodied Bristol VRT 714 (GTX 738W), which was new to National Welsh and was ultimately sold to Brijan, Bishops Waltham, in 1998. (K. A. Jenkinson)

Leaving its stand in Swansea bus station at the start of its journey to Maesteg in April 1991 is Brewer's ex-South Wales Transport Leyland National OEP 789R. (K. A. Jenkinson)

Looking smart as it rests in Swansea bus station in May 1992 is South Wales Transport ECW-bodied Bristol VRT 975 (BEP 975V), which, after being withdrawn in October 1990 and reinstated a month later, was withdrawn again in March 1991 and then returned to service yet again in July of that year. (K. A. Jenkinson)

New in June 1988, Newport Transport's Nipper-branded MCW Metrorider 37 (E37 UBO) was, as can be seen here, fitted with dual-purpose seats. (K. A. Jenkinson)

Starting life with London Buses in June 1987, MCW Metrorider D475 PON was acquired by Parfitts, Rhymney Bridge, in June 1992 and is seen here, a month later, attending a bus rally. (F. W. York)

Freshly repainted in the new Red & White livery, and pictured in Cardiff bus station in January 1992, is Leyland National 410 (KDW 356P), which began life with Western Welsh in December 1975. (K. A. Jenkinson)

Carrying Cityrunner branding, and having arrived at Cardiff bus station on the X2 service from Porthcawl in January 1992, is South Wales Transport Willowbrook-bodied Leyland Leopard 107 (LCY 107X), which was new in January 1982. (K. A. Jenkinson)

Still wearing the livery of its previous owner, Yorkshire Rider, and seen here in Cardiff bus station in January 1992, is Golden Coaches', Llantwit Major, Plaxton-bodied Leyland Leopard LUG 518P. (K. A. Jenkinson)

New to Merthyr Tydfil Transport, Leyland Lynx 53 (E115 SDW) is pictured here after passing to Cynon Valley Transport in whose attractive livery it is seen in Cardiff bus station in February 1992. (K. A. Jenkinson)

Seen in Cardiff bus station in January 1992 is Rhondda Plaxton-bodied Leyland Tiger 904 (AAL 587A), which began life with National Welsh in June 1983 registered SDW 920Y. (K. A. Jenkinson)

According to the label in its windscreen, this bus is 'On hire to Rhondda'. Leyland National ND425 (NOW 459R), pictured here in Cardiff bus station in January 1992, wears National Welsh livery and fleet names but also carries a Rhondda name below its windscreen. (K. A. Jenkinson)

New to Grey Green in September 1980, Duple-bodied Leyland Leopard 98 (FYX 822W) is seen here after its acquisition by Inter Valley Link. (K. A. Jenkinson)

Wearing branding for the X2 service, and seen here entering Cardiff bus station in February 1992, is National Welsh ECW-bodied Bristol VRT LD713 (BUH 238V), which later in the year passed to Morris, Pencoed, was then preserved from 2004 to 2007 before being acquired by Chepstow Classic Buses, and ultimately sold for scrap in March 2012. (K. A. Jenkinson)

New to National Express North East in April 1981, Plaxton-bodied Leyland Leopard U150 (JWE 250W) is seen here in Swansea in June 1992 after transferring to United Welsh Coaches. It later passed to Brian Isaac Coaches. (K. A. Jenkinson)

Cardiff Bus MCW Metrorider 137 (E137 SNY), with Cardiff Clipper Bus branding, stands in front of all-over advertising liveried (except for its front) Alexander-bodied Bristol VRT 361 (WTG 361T). (K. A. Jenkinson)

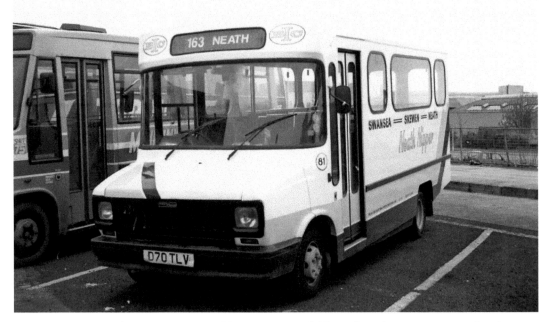

Seen in Swansea bus station in May 1992 wearing Neath Nipper branding is Brian Isaac Coaches Carlyle-bodied Freight Rover Sherpa D70 TLV. Starting life with North Western in Liverpool, after its sale by Brian Isaac to Flying Banana, Great Yarmouth, it was converted to open-top configuration. (K. A. Jenkinson)

Parked in Swansea bus station in June 1992 together with other South Wales Transport buses is ECW-bodied Leyland Olympian 905 (C905 FCY), which had been purchased new by the company in September 1985. (K. A. Jenkinson)

Cwmbran-based Capitol Coaches Plaxton-bodied Leyland Tiger F21 CWO is seen here preparing to undertake a private hire duty in March 1992. (K. A. Jenkinson)

Pictured in Swansea on the 98 service to Gorseinon in June 1992 is Hawkes Coaches City Connection Alexander-bodied Seddon Pennine 7 NSJ 13R, which was new to Western SMT in August 1976. (K. A. Jenkinson)

New to South Wales Transport, ECW-bodied Bristol VRT 975 (BEP 975V) is seen here in Blaen-y-Maes, Swansea, in 1993 painted in The Original Big Red Bus livery, later operated for Paritrans, Northfleet, in 1998, then passed to Grierson, Fishburn, in 1999, and was withdrawn in 2003. (K. A. Jenkinson)

Starting life with Eastern Counties in April 1978 and passing to Tyne & Wear Omnibus Co in February 1989, ECW-bodied Bristol LH6L WEX 931S was later acquired by South Wales Transport for use in its Skillplace Training driving school, with whom it is seen here. (T. W. W. Knowles)

New to Islwyn Borough Transport in September 1981, Marshall-bodied Leyland Leopard GAX 138W was later sold to Pullman, Crofty, with whom it is seen in Swansea bus station in April 1993. It was later disposed of to an operator in Ireland. (K. A. Jenkinson)

Making no secret of its ownership, Brewers ECW-bodied Bristol VRT 949 (UAR 598W) is seen here in Cardiff bus station on the X1 service to Swansea in August 1993. New to Eastern National in June 1981, it then passed to Thamesway in July 1990, United Welsh in April 1992, and Brewers in August 1992. (K. A. Jenkinson)

Still wearing South Wales Transport livery but displaying Brewers fleet names, Leyland National 792 (OEP 792R), seen in Swansea bus station in 1993, had been new to SWT in February 1977. (K. A. Jenkinson)

Making its way through Cardiff en route to Blackwood and Tredegar in 1993 is Islwyn Borough Transport East Lancs-bodied Leyland Tiger 43 (C43 GKG), which was new in November 1985. (K. A. Jenkinson)

New to South Yorkshire PTE in February 1981, after passing to Rhondda Buses, 861 (JHE 156W) is seen here in Cardiff bus station in August 1993. Later, it was sold to MTL, Liverpool, and then passed to Capital Citybus in 1996. (K. A. Jenkinson)

Recently withdrawn National Welsh East Lancs-bodied Dennis Lancets DS495 (A35 XBO and DS497 (A37 XBO), both of which were new to Taff Ely Transport, await their sale to Vanguard, Bedworth, in 1993. (K. A. Jenkinson)

Seen in Cardiff operating a stage carriage service in April 1993 is Rees & Williams twenty-year-old Plaxton-bodied Leyland Leopard UTH 674L, followed by a South Wales Transport Mercedes Benz minibus fitted with roof-mounted advertising boards. (K. A. Jenkinson)

Purchased new by Jones, Pontypridd, in October 1989, and seen here in Cardiff bus station in August 1993 wearing Shamrock Shoppa fleet names, is Duple-bodied Dennis Javelin G847 VAY. (K. A. Jenkinson)

Passing to Brewers in September 1992 but still wearing the livery of South Wales Transport to whom it was new in February 1980, Bristol VRT 973 (BEP 973V), seen here in Swansea bus station in August 1993, passed to Thomas, Porth, in September 1994, and was ultimately scrapped in 2002. (K. A. Jenkinson)

New to National Welsh in May 1980 reregistered BUH 223V and fitted with a Plaxton body, this Leyland Leopard was given a new Plaxton body in December 1987 and reregistered AAL 423A. Here it is seen in Cardiff bus station in April 1994 after being acquired by Porthcawl Omnibus Company. (K. A. Jenkinson)

Awaiting its next duty to Brecon, Marshall-bodied Dennis Dart L414 SFL, seen here in Merthyr Tydfil bus station in May 1994, had been purchased new by local operator Howarth (Silverline) in February of that year. (K. A. Jenkinson)

Seen in Swansea in April 1994 is South Wales Transport Plaxton-bodied Dennis Lance 817 (L817 HCY), which displays its owner, Badgerline's, logo behind its rear wheel arch. (K. A. Jenkinson)

New to Eastern National in April 1983, and seen here in May 1994 on the outskirts of Swansea after being acquired by Brewers, is Alexander-bodied Leyland Tiger 183 (HHJ 379Y). (K. A. Jenkinson)

Starting life as a Carlyle demonstrator, Carlyle-converted Freight Rover Sherpa D283 OOK is seen here on a local service in Cwmbran on 16 March 1994, in the ownership of Phil Anslow Travel. (K. A. Jenkinson)

Seen in Merthyr Tydfil bus station in April 1994 is local independent John's Travel's Wadham Stringer-bodied Ford R1114 OHV 199Y, which had started life with Greater London Council in November 1982. (K. A. Jenkinson)

Leaving Merthyr Tydfil bus station with a full load of passengers in April 1994 is John's Travel Ford Transit taxi-bus F544 JRO, which was new in October 1988. (K. A. Jenkinson)

John's Travel's ex-Yorkshire Rider Carlyle-converted Freight Rover Sherpa D739 JUB is pictured here alongside one of Parfitt's former London Buses Leyland Nationals as it arrives in Merthyr Tydfil bus station in April 1994. (K. A. Jenkinson)

Seen operating the 633 service to West Cross Lane, Swansea, in June 1994 is Howells of Deri's nicely presented ex-London Transport Park Royal-bodied Daimler Fleetline GHV 48N. (K. A. Jenkinson)

Starting life as an Iveco Ford demonstrator in May 1992, Marshall-bodied Iveco 59.12 J228 OKX is seen here in Swansea on hire to D Coaches, Morriston, in April 1994. (K. A. Jenkinson)

One of a number of ex-London Buses Leyland Nationals purchased by Parfitt's, Rhymney Bridge, Volvo-reengined BYW 430V is pictured here unloading its passengers in Merthyr Tydfil bus station in April 1994. (K. A. Jenkinson)

With a Badgerline motif behind its rear wheel arch, and City Mini branding on its side panels, South Wales Transport Plaxton-bodied Dennis Dart 550 (L550 JEP) is seen here in Swansea bus station in July 1994. (K. A. Jenkinson)

Pictured in Stratford-upon-Avon on 11 August 1994 operating a Red & White tour is Waddons of Caerphilly's Plaxton-bodied DAF MB200 PJI 4657, which was new to the company in January 1983 registered RKG 121Y. (K. A. Jenkinson)

Starting life with D Coaches, Morriston, in October 1992, Alexander-bodied Dennis Dart 399 (K82 BWN) is seen here in Swansea in 1995 sporting Rees & Williams identity after becoming part of FirstBus subsidiary South Wales Transport. Alongside it is Brewers Bristol VRT 982 (BEP 982V), also still in SWT livery. (K. A. Jenkinson)

Passing through Bulwark on 16 March 1994 is Stagecoach South Wales Alexander-bodied Mercedes Benz L608D 285 (C808 SDY), which had begun life with Hastings & District in March 1986. (K. A. Jenkinson)

Having just departed from Cwmbran bus station on 16 March 1994, Red & White Carlyle-converted Freight Rover Sherpa 258 (C108 HKG) dated from March 1986. (K. A. Jenkinson)

Passing Cwmbran bus station on 16 March 1994 on local service 2 is Red & White Carlyle-bodied Freight Rover Sherpa 203 (F203 YKG), which was new in August 1988. (K. A. Jenkinson)

Representing Red & White in Cwmbran bus station on 16 March 1994 are Carlyle-bodied
Freight Rover Sherpa 200 (F200 YKG), ex-North Devon Dormobile-bodied Ford Transit 247
(C362 GFJ), ECW-bodied Bristol VRT 707 (BUH 232V), and an unidentified Leyland National.
(K. A. Jenkinson)

New to Merthyr Tydfil Transport in July 1981 and seen here in Merthyr Tydfil bus station in
April 1994 after being acquired by Parfitt's, Rhymney Bridge, is Duple-bodied Leyland Leopard
JUH 231W. (K. A. Jenkinson)

Starting life with Alder Valley, and seen here in Merthyr Tydfil bus station after its purchase by Parfitt's, Rhymney Bridge, is Plaxton-bodied Leyland Leopard GGM 73W, which according to the board in its windscreen is operating the 8 service to Bryngolau. (K. A. Jenkinson)

Resting in Merthyr Tydfil bus station in April 1994 are two Leyland Nationals and an MCW Metrorider, all ex-London Buses, and a former Merthyr Tydfil Transport Duple-bodied Leyland Leopard, each of which are operated by Parfitt's, Rhymney Bridge. (K. A. Jenkinson)

Entering Merthyr Tydfil bus station in April 1994 is Red & White Northern Counties-bodied Renault S56 14 (E929 UBO), which had started life with Cynon Valley Transport in July 1988. (K. A. Jenkinson)

New to Bristol Omnibus Company in March 1986, Dormobile-bodied Ford Transit C434 BHY is seen here in Merthyr Tydfil bus station after passing to Red & White, by whom it was numbered 267. (K. A. Jenkinson)

With Badgerline's smiling badger logo behind its rear wheel arch, and City Mini branding on its side panels, South Wales Transport Plaxton-bodied Dennis Dart 523 (L523 HCY) reverses off the stand in Swansea bus station while operating the Townhill Circular White Route in February 1994. (K. A. Jenkinson)

New to Bristol Omnibus Co. in November 1961, convertible open-top ECW-bodied Bristol FS6G 868 NHT is seen here after being acquired by Smith (Welsh Dragon), Newport, for use on a town tour and private hire duties. (Showbus)

New to Smiths Happiways, Wigan, in May 1982, Duple-bodied Ford R1114 TND 110X is seen here in Swansea after its acquisition by Arthur Thomas Coaches, Gorseinon, who continued trading until 2007. (K. A. Jenkinson)

Seen in Swansea bus station in April 1996 painted in South Wales Transport Shuttle livery, Duple 425 132 (ACY 178A) carries Swansea to Bath route branding at the top of its side windows. (K. A. Jenkinson)

Collecting its passengers in Cardiff bus station in August 1996 is Shamrock Shoppa-liveried Marshall-bodied Dennis Dart N463 OTX, which was new to its owner, Clayton Jones, Pontypridd, in December 1995. (K. A. Jenkinson)

Seen here operating a stage carriage service is Pullman Coaches of Crofty's Plaxton-bodied Leyland Leopard IIB 9890, which was new in February 1980 and sold to an Irish operator in 1996. (K. A. Jenkinson)

Morris Travel's, Carmarthen, Duple-bodied DAF MB230 HIL 7542 is pictured here in Cardiff picking up its private hire passengers in April 1996. (K. A. Jenkinson)

National Welsh ECW-bodied Bristol VRT HR819 (VHB 679S) is seen here in Cardiff bus station in April 1996 sporting Rhondda identity below its destination screen and an 'On Hire to Rhondda' label in its windscreen. After its sale by Rhondda in February 1992, it passed through six further owners before being exported to Holland in August 2018. (K. A. Jenkinson)

Heading along St Mary Street, Cardiff, in April 1996 is Thomas Motors of Barry's freshly repainted Leyland National AKU 165T, which began life with South Yorkshire PTE in March 1979. (K. A. Jenkinson)

Passing through Ravenhill, Swansea, in January 1996 is Hawkes', Waunarlwydd, Leyland National JTH 769P, which was new to South Wales Transport in April 1976. (K. A. Jenkinson)

Awaiting its passengers in Swansea in January 1996 when only a few days old is Jones of Login's Plaxton-bodied Dennis Javelin N390 KDE. (K. A. Jenkinson)

Seen in Swansea in September 1996 is Brian Isaac Coaches ex-Yorkshire Rider Roe-bodied Leyland Fleetline CWU 147T, which was new to West Yorkshire PTE in September 1978. After leaving South Wales, it was exported to Toronto, Canada, where it was converted to open-top configuration for use on sightseeing tours. (K. A. Jenkinson)

Seen elsewhere in this book, Rees & Williams Alexander-bodied Dennis Dart K92 BWN is pictured here in Swansea in 1996 wearing its original livery and sporting a Dyfed Diamonds fleet name. (K. A. Jenkinson)

New to Eastern National in June 1981, and later passing to Thamesway before reaching United Welsh in December 1991, Brewers ECW-bodied Bristol VRT UAR 587W is seen here in Swansea in September 1996 wearing a free bus livery on behalf of Asda. In 2001, it was, however, exported to an unknown destination. (K. A. Jenkinson)

In Cardiff bus station on 12 April 1997 awaiting its next journey to Blackwood and Tredegar, Islwyn Borough Transport East Lancs-bodied Leyland Tiger 46 (D46 MBO) was new to the undertaking in October 1986. (K. A. Jenkinson)

New to Rhymney Valley DC in November 1982 and seen here with Inter Valley Link is East Lancs-bodied Leyland Leopard 89 (PWO 89Y). (K. A. Jenkinson)

Jones of Pontypridd's Shamrock Shoppa-liveried Northern Counties-bodied Dennis Lance P224 WBV is seen entering Cardiff bus station on 12 April 1997. (K. A. Jenkinson)

Seen in Cardiff bus station on 12 April 1997 is Alison Jones-owned Thomas of Barry's P225 WBV, a Northern Counties-bodied Dennis Lance new in November 1996. (K. A. Jenkinson)

Entering Cardiff bus station on 12 April 1997 is FirstBus subsidiary, Brewers, Duple-bodied Leyland Tiger 163 (EWR 654Y), which had been transferred from First West Yorkshire and had been new to West Yorkshire PTE in June 1983. (K. A. Jenkinson)

Seen at its owner's depot in April 1997 is Islwyn Borough Transport's East Lancs-bodied Dodge G08 midibus 48 (D406 NUH), which dated from April 1987. (K. A. Jenkinson)

Starting life with Alexander Fife in January 1980, Leyland National 2 RSG 821V stands alongside ex-Ribble Leyland National CBV 790S at their owner's, Glyn Williams, Crosskeys depot on 12 April 1997. (K. A. Jenkinson)

Purchased new by Islwyn Borough Transport in December 1995, Plaxton-bodied Mercedes Benz 811D 12 (N573 OUH) is seen in its owner's depot yard in April 1997. (K. A. Jenkinson)

Plaxton Derwent-bodied Leyland Leopard UJX 918M was new to Halifax Corporation in December 1973, and after passing to West Yorkshire PTE in 1974 and Maynes, Manchester, in 1986, it was acquired from Golden Coaches by Glyn Williams, Crosskeys, in whose yard it is seen here in April 1997 with a 'Convoy of Hope, Wales-Croatia' sticker on its lower front panel. (K. A. Jenkinson)

Seen in Merthyr Tydfil bus station on 12 April 1997 is Parfitt's, Rhymney Bridge, Plaxton-bodied Dennis Dart 62 (N62 MTG), which had been purchased new in October 1995. (K. A. Jenkinson)

Pulling out of Dan Bryn Avenue, Radyr, and wearing Cardiff Bus's new livery, is East Lancs-bodied Leyland Olympian 560 (C560 GWO), which was new in March 1986. (K. A. Jenkinson)

Bought new in October 1996 by Jones, Pontypridd, Alexander Dash-bodied Dennis Dart P122DMS, with Shamrock Shoppa fleet names, stands in Cardiff bus station in April 1997. (K. A. Jenkinson)

Much-travelled Duple 300-bodied Leyland Tiger A17RBL began life with Jim Stones, Glazebury, in August 1988, registered F311 RMH, and was then operated by Whitelaw, Stonehouse and Kelvin Central Buses before joining Rhondda Buses in 1994. Here it is seen in Cardiff bus station on 12 April 1997. (K. A. Jenkinson)

Seen at its owner's depot in April 1997, Islwyn Borough Transport Willowbrook-bodied Leyland Leopard 5 (LBO 729P) was new to the undertaking in January 1976. (K. A. Jenkinson)

Starting life with Evans, New Tredegar, in April 1982, Plaxton-bodied Bedford YNT 83 (WBC 940X) is seen here in April 1997 after joining Islwyn Borough Transport's small coach fleet. (K. A. Jenkinson)

New to Peter Sheffield, Cleethorpes, in May 1987, registered D512 WNV, Caetano-bodied DAF MB230 was sold to Islwyn Borough Transport in 1988 and reregistered IIL 7331, and is seen here in April 1997 wearing its new owner's Kingfisher coach livery. (K. A. Jenkinson)

Resting at the Pembroke Dock depot of its new owner, Silcox, in March 1997, well-presented Alexander-bodied Leyland Leopard MHS 19P had begun life with Central SMT in March 1976. (K. A. Jenkinson)

Silcox's, Pembroke Dock, Duple-bodied Bristol LH6L 141 (LDE 166P), seen here in March 1997, was purchased new by its owner in May 1976 and continued in service until 2003, after which it was scrapped. (K. A. Jenkinson)

Starting life with West Riding Automobile Co. in March 1975 fitted with an Alexander coach body, in October 1988 Leyland Leopard HWY 719N was sold to South Wales independent Glyn Williams, who immediately fitted it with a new Willowbrook Warrior body, and later sold it to Silcox, Pembroke Dock, with whom it is seen here in March 1997. (K. A. Jenkinson)

Resting in the yard of its owner, Silcox, Pembroke Dock, in March 1997 is ECW-bodied Bristol VRT AJA 421L, which was ordered by North Western but entered service with SELNEC, Manchester, in July 1973, and then passed to Stevensons, Uttoxeter, in 1984 before being acquired in 1987 by Silcox, who continued to operate it until 1997, after which it was scrapped. (K. A. Jenkinson)

New to South Yorkshire PTE in February 1980, but acquired by Silcox from Camms, Nottingham, Roe-bodied Leyland Atlantean CWG 707V is seen at Pembroke Dock in March 1997. (K. A. Jenkinson)

Painted in National Express Airlink livery and arriving at Newport bus station on its way to Gatwick airport on 12 April 1997 is South Wales Transport's two-year old Plaxton-bodied Dennis Javelin 111 (M111 PWN). (K. A. Jenkinson)

Registered YR3 939 when new to Yorkshire Rider in April 1988 and seen here in Cardiff in April 1997 after its transfer to FirstBus United Welsh Coaches, Jonckheere-bodied Volvo B10M 199 (300 CUH) still wears its original owner's Jet Rider livery. (K. A. Jenkinson)

Richards Bros', Moylgrove, Duple-bodied DAF SB2300 RBO 284 was purchased new by its owner in April 1986 and originally registered C785 CDG. (K. A. Jenkinson)

Seen in its home town bus station in April 1997 is Newport Transport's Alexander-bodied Scania N113CRB 6 (K106 YTX), which was new to the municipal undertaking in March 1993. (K. A. Jenkinson)

Withdrawn at Cardiff Bus's Sloper Road depot in April 1997 after being purchased from Cardiff Bluebird – but not operated – are MCW Metrobuses 53 (JHE 143W) and 51 (JHE 141W), which were new to South Yorkshire PTE in January 1981 and then operated by Motts, Aylesbury, before reaching Cardiff. (K. A. Jenkinson)

Arriving in Newport bus station in April 1997 is Glyn Williams Plaxton-bodied Mercedes Benz 811D 26 (M243 JHB), which had been purchased new in August 1994. (K. A. Jenkinson)

New to Whitelaw, Stonehouse, in August 1991 and then operated by Redby, Sunderland, before being acquired by Rhondda Buses, Leyland Lynx 42 (J42 GGB), seen here in Cardiff bus station on 12 April 1997, ended its life across the water in Ireland with Bus Eireann. (K. A. Jenkinson)

Rhondda Buses Leyland Tiger 703 (A13 RBL) is a bus with an unusual history. Starting life in June 1990 as a prison van registered G399 PNN, it was fitted with a new East Lancs dual-purpose bus body in June 1995, as seen here in Cardiff bus station in September 1997. After its sale by Rhondda, it served with Southlands, Bromley; Bommerang, Tewkesbury; and finally Ogden, St Helens. (K. A. Jenkinson)

New to Stagecoach Red & White in December 1994, Plaxton-bodied Dennis Javelin 943 (M943 JBO), seen here entering Cardiff bus station in September 1997 with bold Stagecoach 2000 lettering on its side panels, was later transferred to Stagecoach Burnley & Pendle. (K. A. Jenkinson)

Operated by Leisurelink on The Cardiff Tour on behalf of Guide Friday, whose livery it wears, is open-top East Lancs-bodied Leyland Atlantean KHC 814K, which had started life in February 1972 as a conventional closed-top bus with Eastbourne Borough Transport and is seen here in Cardiff city centre in September 1997. (K. A. Jenkinson)

New to Western Welsh in April 1971 and later converted into a recovery vehicle, Stagecoach Red & White Willowbrook-bodied Leyland Leopard RW2 (BTX 332J) is seen here at Cwmbran depot on 12 April 1997. (K. A. Jenkinson)

Resting at its owner's Sloper Road depot on 12 April 1997 is Cardiff Bus Alexander-bodied Ailsa B55 439 (A154 HLV), which had been acquired from Merseyside PTE, to whom it was new in June 1984. (K. A. Jenkinson)

New to D Coaches subsidiary, Rees & Williams, Reeve Burgess-bodied Mercedes Benz 811D H853 OWN is seen here in Llanelli in September 1997 painted in South Wales Transport livery with FirstBus R&W logos. (K. A. Jenkinson)

New to Excelsior, Bournemouth, in April 1980, Roberts Coaches Plaxton-bodied Ford R1114 HFX 420V is seen here in Llanelli on a school's duty in September 1997. (K. A. Jenkinson)

Heading through Llanelli in September 1997 is Gwyn Williams ex-Luton & District Dormobile-bodied Freight Rover Sherpa D387 SGS. (K. A. Jenkinson)

Seen in Merthyr Tydfil bus station in 1997 is Stagecoach Red & White Marshall-bodied Mercedes Benz 811D 331 (L331 CHB). (K. A. Jenkinson)

Rhondda Buses subsidiary Parfitt's Marshall-bodied Dennis Dart SLF 56 (P56 XBO), which was new in April 1997, is seen here painted in Caerphilly Busways livery entering Merthyr Tydfil bus station in August 1997. (K. A. Jenkinson)

New to Clydeside Scottish in July 1985 registered B405 OSB, but later reregistered B973 OSB Rhondda Buses Plaxton-bodied Dennis Dorchester 909 is seen here in Merthyr Tydfil bus station in August 1997 painted in dedicated TrawsCambria livery. (K. A. Jenkinson)

Seen in Newport bus station in September 1997 is Stagecoach Red & White Leyland Lynx 397 (E115SDW), which was new to Merthyr Tydfil Transport in January 1988. (K. A. Jenkinson)

In the yard of Stagecoach Red & White's Bulwark (Chepstow) depot on 12 April 1997 is Alexander-bodied Bristol VRT 861 (OSR 206R), which was new to Tayside in March 1977. It had been purchased by National Welsh in 1981 and was ultimately scrapped in July 1998. Alongside it is ex-Stagecoach Busways Alexander-bodied Leyland Atlantean 870 (AVK 173V), which began life with Tyne & Wear PTE in July 1980. (K. A. Jenkinson)

Looking rather scruffy as it stands in Newport bus station in September 1997 is Stagecoach Red & White ECW-bodied Bristol VRT 833 (DBV 26W), which had transferred from Ribble in April 1994 and was withdrawn and sold to a non-PSV user in Ulster in December 1998. (K. A. Jenkinson)

Wadham Stringer was an unusual choice by municipal undertakings as a body builder for their conventional size single-deckers, but Newport Transport selected it for its nine Scania BR112DHs placed in service in March 1983. One of these buses, 10 (RUH 10Y), is seen here in its hometown bus station in September 1997. (K. A. Jenkinson)

New in December 1996 as a UVG demonstrator, and seen here in Newport bus station in September 1997 with Glyn Williams, who ultimately purchased it, is UVG-bodied Dennis Dart SLF P423 PBP, which, after passing to Stagecoach with the Glyn Williams business, was fitted with a Plaxton Pointer front. (K. A. Jenkinson)

Circumnavigating Newport bus station in September 1997 is Stagecoach Duple-bodied Dennis Javelin F243 OFP, which was new to Whites Travel, Calver, in March 1989, and is seen here branded for the Newport–Cheltenham 73 service. (K. A. Jenkinson)

Pictured in Swansea bus station in March 1997 painted in South Wales Transport livery with added FirstBus logos is Plaxton-bodied Dennis Dart 576 (P576 BTH), which was new in October 1996. (K. A. Jenkinson)

Seen in Swansea in March 1997, looking shabby, is Rees & Williams Alexander-bodied Leyland Tiger WAO 644Y which began life with Cumberland in March 1983, and then passed to Lancaster City Transport, before reaching South Wales. (K. A. Jenkinson)

Posed for the camera at Stagecoach Red & White's Cwmbran depot on 12 April 1997 is Northern Counties-bodied Leyland Atlantean 871 (VBA 166S), which was new to Greater Manchester PTE in February 1978, and still displays the logo of its previous operator, Greater Manchester South, in its front nearside upper-deck window. (K. A. Jenkinson)

Stagecoach's standard conventional-size single-decker in the 1990s was the Alexander PS-bodied Volvo B10M, as seen here with Red & White 768 (M768 RAX) in Newport bus station on 12 April 1997. (K. A. Jenkinson)